Wood
Carving

Alan Durst ANNUNCIATION Yew wood, 2 feet 2 inches high
Detail of carving appears on jacket

Wood Carving

Alan Durst

A Studio Book

THE VIKING PRESS • New York

TO MY WIFE
for all her help

First published in Great Britain by The Studio Limited, now Studio Vista
Limited, London
Issued in the U.S.A. in 1969 by The Viking Press, Inc. 625 Madison Avenue,
New York N.Y. 10022
Library of Congress catalog card number 69-10593
Printed and bound in the Netherlands

CONTENTS

ILLUSTRATIONS

EXAMPLES OF WOOD-CARVING

Grateful acknowledgment is made to artists who have kindly lent examples of their work for reproduction. The author wishes to make special acknowledgment to R. Dufton Esq, for the skill and patience with which he photographed the carvings in progress.

PREFACE TO THE THIRD EDITION

It is twenty years since this book was first published; and ten years since the issue of a revised edition.

Between 1938–48 everything to do with art and craftsmanship was deeply affected by World War II and its attendant circumstances. Yet I doubt whether that upheaval caused so much fundamental change and unrest in the general outlook on the visual arts as has the subsequent decade.

The Atomic Age—the Cold War—fear and the disrupting influences at work everywhere, are reflected in the troubled spirit which increasingly divides the art world into two factions—neither of which is prepared to recognize the validity of the other.

On the one side art is objective—based on the interpretation of nature; on the other it is largely subjective—holding itself free to develop in any way out of the sub-consciousness of the individual artist.

The former is as old as pre-history; the latter is new—and news.

As a consequence of this the latter has by far the better Press at the present time, which makes it attractive to some students and young artists who want to follow the fashion, without having thought very deeply about the matter.

Objective art becomes sterile when an artist turns only to traditional art for inspiration, instead of constantly renewing his vision from experience.

Subjective art can too easily get bogged down in doodling and self-deception.

But, setting aside the extremists on both sides (who are probably hopeless in any case), should there not be a wide field of common ground where all artists and amateurs of good will can meet without controversy?

To learn and master his craft so that it literally becomes a part of his nature, setting him free to express his thoughts unhampered, is one of the rewards of an artist's life. Painting, engraving, modelling, carving, each has its special paraphernalia and equipment—and its special skill. Skill is the key word; for art originally implied skill; and without the intelligent use of his skill, I do not think that any artist can truly delight in his work.

Doodling and messing about with chancy and accidental effects may, perhaps, afford fun for a while; but chance and accident are poor substitutes for that ability to do the job well which has characterized the practice of art through the ages. Every beginner who thinks about it will come to agree.

Recently at an important meeting concerned with the subject of handicrafts, I heard it said that in this age of machine-tools we must be realistic and not try to 'throw our hats against the wind': that we should not expect, or even encourage, any interest in handicraftsmanship. The speaker considered for instance that the working of wood was becoming obsolete. This, very briefly, is the challenge that must be met. The danger, as I see it, is nothing less than the decline and disappearance of the visual arts from the human scene—for how long can they exist if their roots are cut away?

This could happen—and should it happen, would it matter if science and engineering took its place?

To my mind nothing could take its place. And mankind without art—as without religion—would be without order or direction.

For there is a mystical quality about the creative work of a man's hands which defies analysis. Few artists know just how the thing happens; and it is a matter of common experience for an artist to feel that he is a channel through which a mind outside of himself is finding expression.

It is this vital force, reaching down through every degree of work where the hands are carrying out a creative design, which must be sustained and recognized if humanity is to win in the great issue with which it is faced—the war between Materialism and the things of the Spirit.

Some extreme forms of contemporary art may seem to turn their backs on traditional materials and traditional craftsmanship; but I believe we are justified in looking on this as a passing phase.

Consider the arts in general. It is unlikely, to say the least of it, for them to be out of step for long. Literature and Drama—after a few abortive attempts to go 'queer'—remain true to their historic past in their outlook on the future. While the crowded audiences at the Old Vic and Covent Garden surely witness that human nature is universally the same today as yesterday. Indeed, *Hamlet* and *Swan Lake* typify almost the only safe bridge across the political gulf which divides the world.

Traditional Art is not dead. But it has powerful and cynical forces ranged against it which must be combated wherever and whenever possible.

This then is the justification and the added need for the continued publication of any one of the handbooks on the technique of the arts.

The need is there; the opportunities and openings are there also for those who, having faith in themselves, care to learn 'how to do it'.

Alan Durst, 1959

PREFACE TO THE 1948 EDITION

This book was written in 1938. It seems natural, therefore, in revising it for a new edition to take stock of how its subject has been affected by the eventful years which have passed since its first publication.

The following are, perhaps, the most obvious points, favourable and unfavourable, which call for consideration.

First: Throughout the war years in all the belligerent countries there has been the inevitable slowing down, almost to stopping-point in some instances, of the arts of peace.

Secondly: There has been an increased interest taken in the arts generally; an interest partly evoked no doubt by a revulsion from all the waste and destruction which have been going on in the world. This has led also to an eagerness on the part of many—especially, perhaps, the men and women in the services—to learn the practice of some art for themselves.

Thirdly: There has been, and still is in Britain at any rate, a hampering lack of the tools and materials with which to carry on almost every art, not least that of wood-carving. These conditions will no doubt gradually right themselves.

Fourthly: There have been since the end of the war hopeful signs in some quarters of a growing and more intelligent demand for the work of artists in general.

Lastly: Throughout most of Europe there has been the lamentable destruction of works of art of all kinds, in which destruction nothing has been more vulnerable than wood-carvings. In London this latter loss has been most deplorable; and one object of the revised illustrations in the 1948 edition of this book has been to give some idea of the treasures of seventeenth-century carving which have perished in the blitz. No doubt we had grown to look upon our heritage as permanent and to treat it as a matter of course. Perhaps now, when much that is irreplaceable has been lost for ever and more has been damaged or threatened, our appreciation will have been quickened by the realization of the insecurity of our hold on the works of past ages, which too often we have squandered and neglected. If this should indeed be the case, our loss may yet lead to some gain; for an awakened knowledge of the arts of former times and an understanding of their place in the lives of the people may well stimulate the right demand for contemporary work.

For an art, to be really alive, must grow in its natural soil; without roots it can have no more continuity or permanence than cut flowers in a vase. The soil in which the sculptor's art in every country has flourished has been formed principally of the materials of that country.

In Britain these materials are stone and timber; and it is in a variety of stones and woods that the true native sculpture of these islands has been made in the past—in none perhaps more conspicuously than in English oak.

I am not, of course, suggesting that imported materials ever have been, or should be, banned altogether. The twelfth-century English carvings in ivory, for instance, are among the loveliest things of their kind. But such exceptions do not affect the main argument that an art must be concerned with local conditions if it is to be of more than local significance.

The roofs and screens of the fifteenth century in East Anglia and the wood-carvings of Wren's churches were only made possible by the concerted efforts of a number of men working to one end and forming a school. There were, of course, differences in stature among individuals; but the direction was clear to all, and each man's work could be measured and judged by a recognized and accepted standard.

The level attained by a school whose work is meeting the needs of a community must be higher than that reached by an individual working on his own account; and it is from the high level of combined effort and singleness of purpose that the finest works of the past have arisen.

To many people the visual arts would seem to be in a valley at the present time. They lack unity and direction; they are disrupted by conceit and excessive individualism, which may set a fashion but can never found a school.

The art world is divided into sects which dislike each other. The extreme groups on either side have diverged far from the tradition of which each assumes the trusteeship. And with a vociferousness which possibly betrays some lurking doubt, each side claims to be the only representative of art worth considering.

Between the two, a bewildered public, knowing that both sides cannot be right, may be forgiven if it suspects that neither is the sole repository of the Truth!

There is, however, a middle group of artists—conspicuous neither for their salesmanship nor their advertising ability—whose work has small news value for the very reason that it truly is traditional. It aims at interpreting nature in the idiom of its own age; as traditional art always has done since man first discovered the means of expressing himself through sculpture and painting.

If a genuine, unspectacular revival of art is possible at the present time, it must surely start from the wider employment of this central body of art-workers on worthwhile jobs.

The matter rests partly on the discrimination of those who have the work to offer. It rests also with the workmen. If sculptors and students will turn their hands increasingly towards their native materials—not least their native timbers—they will go some way towards encouraging the right demand for their work which they and the community at large so greatly need.

Alan Durst, 1948

Introduction

Carving, or sculpture, is known to have been one of the very earliest activities of man. Thousands of years before he knew anything of agriculture or clothing, of ordered building or settled living, he had found a way of chipping and rubbing and scraping a variety of materials into shapes.

Carvings in bone and horn and ivory have survived from, perhaps, 30,000 years ago—carvings which for sculptural feeling have, in some instances, scarcely been surpassed throughout the whole subsequent history of art. Naturally all woodwork of anything approaching this age must long since have perished: but common sense and the analogy of all primitive races tell us that when bone and ivory were carved, wood of all kinds must also have been carved, and on a more extensive scale.

A realization of the immense antiquity of the art of carving should help to emphasize its significance in the development and culture of the human race. Obviously the need of carving and what carving expresses must be fundamental to our nature. It would be out of place to enlarge on this theme to any extent in the short introduction to a technical hand-book. But, very briefly, I would like to suggest that the key to that need may be found in the word 'order'. The artist tries to interpret life in terms of order: to hold some one aspect of the ever-changing and bewildering vision around him in a permanent design: to find harmony amid confusion: to discover a resting-place for the mind. The search for order is ultimately the search for truth.

From the very beginning down through all the ages, human society has found practical uses to which the work of the artist could be put; to the incalculable enrichment of the whole world and the vital interest of the artist himself. But since the industrial revolution of last century conditions have changed, and the artist no longer functions naturally and inevitably as a working part of a social order.

It is probable that the neglect of the wise employment of art on an extensive scale throughout the world has a direct bearing upon the present state of international unrest. The sense of values in the world today is chaotic: and many artists are driven, through economic conditions, to reflect in their work the very distraction which they should be setting at rest. The need for an appreciation, not merely of art, but of the *sanity* which all genuine art expresses can seldom, if ever, have been greater.

13

The number of art students throughout the country, many of them of great promise, is some indication of the persistence of an impulse which is continually trying to find an outlet. That this talent should be absorbed into our common life, and not allowed to run to waste, is a matter which concerns the whole future of our civilization. For only through that way of life which is reflected in the arts shall we ever reach the unity, peace and concord which all men of goodwill desire. We cannot, of course, expect any sudden change; any sensational ushering-in of the millennium. But a real revival may come, when least expected, through a gradual influence working undetected on the minds of men.

A work of art gives out whatever has been put into it. If we could compute the spiritual force which emanates from all the good carving which has been done in the past, it would help each individual carver to realize the importance of the work he is endeavouring to carry on, and the responsibility which rests upon his shoulders.

This then, in my opinion, is the line of thought by which the student who intends to take up wood-carving should approach his work: that all carving is sculpture, and that wood was probably the earliest material to be carved: that the need for order, or harmony, as expressed through carving, is fundamental to human nature: that a recognition of this need is of vital importance to the world at the present time.

To regard wood-carving as sculpture may be new to many who have grown up in the widely accepted idea that sculpture is modelling, and that carving is a humbler activity, done by craftsmen, among whom wood-carvers take the least considerable place.

How, during the last four centuries, this topsy-turvy notion has come into being is too big a question to go into here. But that it is unjustified and unjustifiable on any ground except that of commercial expediency, will scarcely be denied by anyone who has the smallest knowledge of the practice and history of art. Sculpture, as the word denotes, is primarily carving; and modelling is only rightly used for such works as are intended to be cast in metal or fired as terra-cotta. Modelling ought not to form the basis of carving, which should be conceived and carried out in the material itself. In all good carving thought and action are so fused—so interdependent—that it would be out of the question for the designer to delegate to another the execution of his ideas.

This book is intended primarily to help only those who wish to learn to

14

Alan Durst
BEAR CUB
Lignum vitae
Height, 16 inches
Collection T. J. Barnes

carry out their own designs and give expression to their own thoughts through the art of carving wood. This applies not only to the student who is starting on what he means to make his career, but also to the amateur and part-time worker. Under existing conditions, when the output is much greater than the demand, naturally much good work is being done by those who cannot risk giving all their time to the practice of any art.

To do a thing for the love of doing it is the highest motive: and, where there is singleness of purpose, to work as an amateur need not imply any inferiority. Anyone who contrives to fill his life by doing two jobs instead of one, as some artists are doing today, can at least claim the courage of his convictions. It is the standard of work which alone matters.

The actual technique of wood-carving is readily learned by anyone who has natural aptitude and knows one end of a tool from the other. Complete mastery can, of course, come only through constant practice and wide experience; but the tools and implements of wood-carving are so simple, and the process so natural, that the beginner should quickly be able to get into his stride. From my own teaching I have learned the value of this; because at a very early stage the student is able to concentrate his mind not so much upon *how* to carve but upon the far more important questions of *what* to carve, and what are the qualities to be aimed at in good carving. In other words, the manual skill which he acquires can grow naturally in subjection to his development as an artist; and he runs far less risk of making craftsmanship an end in itself than he would do were he compelled to spend much time on exercises whose sole purpose was the teaching of technique. It is my experience that wherever there are ideas to be expressed the necessary technique to express them will always be forthcoming.

In saying this, I am not belittling the importance of technical ability, which is, of course, indispensable in the practice of any art; but I do wish to stress the point that for this ability to be worth anything at all it must wait upon vision and understanding—vision to see life in its essentials, and understanding to interpret life in terms of carved, or sculptured, form. This I believe to be true of all carving, from a simple pattern in relief to work that is fully in the round.

It is undoubtedly true that this vision and understanding have not infrequently been found in those who at first merely felt that they wanted to do something with their hands—perhaps only to find a hobby to occupy their leisure. 'You never know what you can do until you try', is often true of those who are not consciously aware of any creative faculty; and many artists, some of the first rank, would seem to have blundered upon their careers almost by accident. It is for this reason that I would urge anyone who feels drawn to learn wood-carving, in whatever capacity, to start with the idea firmly in his head that design and execution are one and indivisible. No one can possibly design with real understanding that which he is incapable of carving; for only through doing the actual work can he appreciate the character of his material and turn its possibilities and limitations to account. It must be equally obvious that a carver who is content merely to copy, cannot work with the spontaneity and invention which are essential to vital carving, and which make carving worth while.

The reader who has never handled a carving tool may feel that he is being told he cannot begin to carve until he can design for carving, and vice versa— and yet a start has to be made somewhere. Proverbially, first steps are all important: it is equally true that they are the most difficult. A little later, after I have spoken about tools and materials, I shall try, through the example of a simple relief carving described in its progressive stages, to suggest how this start may be made.

In the meantime, before going any further, there is one thing which I would recommend to all who themselves intend to carve, and that is to look at carvings. Many will take this as a matter of course and perhaps feel that they have been doing so all their lives. But if they have not looked with the eye of a potential carver they have not seen carvings in the way I mean. As soon as you make carving your personal concern your point of view will change—it will become more critical. You will try to look backwards and see the wood as it was before it was worked at all: you will consider with new vision how the design fills its allotted space and adapts itself, well or ill, to the nature of the material: you will notice how the treatment which is right for the coarse grain of oak would not do so well for, say, lime-wood: you will look for the marks of the different tools and wonder how the sculptor got his surface finish. And in seeing all this (and much more) you will prepare your mind for doing the job yourself, and unconsciously acquire much knowledge which you will find useful later on.

What carvings to look at and where to look for them must be largely a matter of circumstance and opportunity.

The easiest way to study wood-carvings is in a museum; and for this, in England, the Victoria and Albert Museum is unsurpassed. I do not imagine that anywhere else can there be a more comprehensive collection or one more accessibly displayed. Here European carvings of almost every kind can be examined in detail. Complementary to this are the ethnographical departments of the great museums where, amongst a great many beads and feathers, there may be discovered wonderful examples of the carvings of primitive races —carvings which from their singleness of purpose and directness of technique should be helpful to all discriminating students.

But apart from the museums there is, of course, wood-carving of one sort or another, old or new, to be found almost everywhere. Only be sure of this— whatever you find, whether it be in museum or cathedral, in art gallery or second-hand shop, in village church or modern house, look at it without prejudice and look at it critically. Make up your mind as to whether or not it seems right to you *as carved wood*, accepting nothing by any other standard; condemning nothing for any other reason. Almost everything you see in this way should teach you something about wood-carving.

BULL CALF
Lignum vitae
Length, 14 inches
Glasgow Corporation

Tools and materials

As illustrations of method I have carved two pieces—one a relief in plane-wood, the other a figure in the round in teak.

I have kept a careful record of all the tools I have used in carving these two pieces, and they are shown in the plate on the next page. There are eleven tools shown here, varying in size from 'A' which is one and a quarter inches across, to 'L' which is one-eighth inch. The cut made by each tool is shown just beneath its letter. Actually, all are gouges, though some of them, 'F', 'I' and 'H', are almost flat. But each of these has a very slight curve and is sharpened with a bevel on one side only. 'K' is a very quick gouge, known as a fluter. The shortness of some of the tools is due to their having been broken and re-ground. This in no way impairs their efficiency; except that a long tool is better for the less accessible parts of some carvings.

I do not say that these tools are all that will ever be needed; but they are approximately those which I should recommend for a start. Later, experience will teach what others are required and what are one's own particular preferences. Avoid getting anything which may be described as a carver's outfit. The fewer tools with which one can manage the better. They should be kept in a baize case with a separate division for each tool; and treated with respect. Mallets are usually made of beech-wood or lignum vitae, and those with round heads are the best. The mallet seen on page 26 is of beech-wood with a box-wood handle, and weighs two pounds.

The first thing one must do after buying one's tools is to learn to sharpen them. For this will be needed:

A Washita oilstone.

An India slip.

Various small slips for the insides of the small gouges.

A strop.

A tin of the best machine oil.

The oilstone should be placed on the bench in such a way that it does not move about. Either it may be held in position by a slight recess cut in the bench, about one-eighth inch deep, to fit the stone (not a bad first practice in carving); or by little strips of wood nailed on to the bench close up to the sides of the stone.

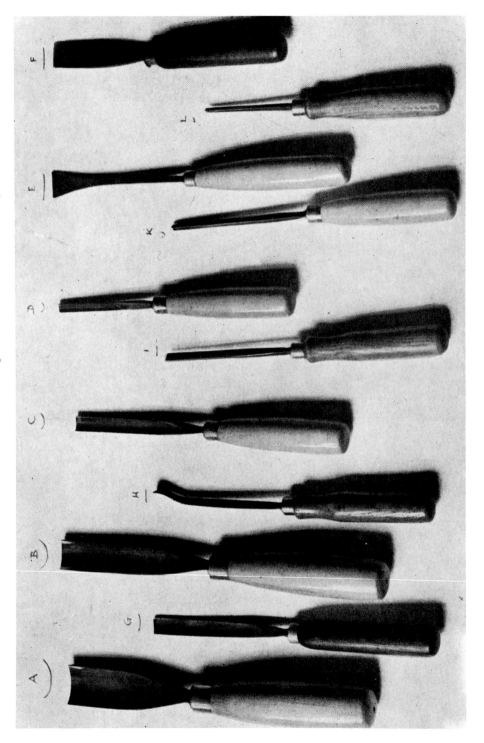

1. These are the tools used in carving the two demonstration carvings

The cut made by each tool is shown just beneath its reference letter

Note: To the tools shown on page 20 I would add two flat tools, say three-quarters to half–inch wide respectively. These are useful on slightly convex surfaces, and for lettering.

Having fixed the stone, drop a little oil on the face. Start with the convex side of one of the flatter gouges (say 'G'). Holding the tool by the handle in the right hand with the fingers of the left hand steadying the blade, place it on the stone in such a position that the bevel lies flat on the surface, and rotate it evenly from side to side with a firm and uniform pressure. Be careful not to press more firmly in one place than another or you will rub angles on the back. Be careful also not to raise the handle, for by working the tool against the stone at too steep an angle you will produce a secondary bevel near the point. Correctly sharpened, the back should have a perfectly uniform smoothness. When this is achieved, feel the inner or concave side with the finger. A very slight burr or roughness will be noticed. Take the India slip and find that part of it where the curve corresponds to the concave side of the tool. Rub the tool gently against the slip so as to remove the burr, but *not* to form a bevel on the inner side. Wipe the tool on a rag, and strop it by drawing the convex side quickly along the leather, with the forefinger of the right hand on the blade and the cutting edge flat on the strop. The strop should be dressed with emery paste. It may be tacked on to the bench; it must always be wiped clean of all grit before use. A small flexible leather, which can be bent round the finger, may be used for stropping the inner sides of the larger gouges.

A straight-edged chisel and a V tool are sharpened in the same way, though the latter needs a fine slip for the inner angle. Both these tools are chiefly required for incised lettering, for which the former is indispensable.

A tool when sharp should cut with a clean bit across the grain of deal.

The oilstone and slips should always be wiped free from oil when work is finished for the day.

Sharp tools are essential to good carving. It is therefore worth while to learn to sharpen them properly; and if great pains are taken with this at the outset one soon acquires the knack of keeping them in condition.

Should a tool get nicked or broken it must be re-ground. Although, here again, there is nothing difficult in the process, a grindstone, if mishandled, can be very destructive to tools. I do not recommend a beginner to attempt to grind his own tools until he has had an opportunity of seeing for himself how it should be done. I shall not, therefore, attempt to describe the process; but I would advise everyone, when first he has tools to be ground, to take them to a professional wood-carver or toolsmith and to ask for a practical demonstration. It will be time enough then for him to think of buying a grindstone of his own.

SUITABLE WOODS

There are a great number of woods which are suitable for carving; each one of which has its own characteristics. The following is a list of some of the most usual and useful.

Oak: in England oak is used more than any other wood; and it deserves its place on account of its strength, its colour and its lovely grain. It requires a broad treatment and is tough to carve, particularly the English variety. Austrian oak is straighter in grain and cuts more easily. Japanese oak is not such a satisfactory wood.

Walnut: American walnut is a very good, hard wood, with a close and even grain. English walnut is equally good but more difficult to get. Italian walnut is an excellent wood; slightly harder than the others but not so dark in colour.

Mahogany: this is a lovely wood to carve. It is moderately hard, and varies in colour from golden brown to a rich dark red.

Teak: a very strong wood with much the same characteristics as oak. It is the best of all woods for weathering out of doors. It carves beautifully though it is blunting for the tools.

Lime: a soft, light wood, which cuts easily and has an even grain.

Sycamore: a white wood, tougher than lime and less pleasant to carve.

Birch: a very good medium-hard wood with a pleasant grain and colour.

Plane: much the same, with a more pronounced 'figure' in it.

Pine: at its best can be carved. It requires very broad, free treatment and very sharp tools, and is, consequently, an excellent material upon which to practice.

Pear: cuts beautifully and is unsurpassed for small and delicate work.

American Bass-wood: a medium wood of even grain and unattractive colour. It can be obtained in large sizes and is nice to carve. It is particularly suitable for work to be coloured or gilded.

Jarrah: from Australia. A hard, red wood which carves very evenly.

Lignum vitae, Ebony, Snake-wood and other very hard tropical woods require their own methods of working and treatment. They should not be tackled by anyone who has not already gained a certain amount of experience through carving more ordinary woods.

22

Wood can be bought from a carpenter's or joiner's shop, or from a timber merchant. In the latter case a friendly foreman will generally let one hunt through his stock for suitable pieces, and will often set aside the sort of thing which he thinks a regular client may require. You must be able to trust your man to sell you wood which he knows to be properly seasoned. Timber in balk takes many years to season, and its history must be known. Do not use wood from trees which you know to have been cut down recently; or to have fallen from natural causes. To season properly, timber should be felled at the appropriate time of year. In most cases this is in the autumn when the sap is down.

However careful you may be over your selection, in wood of any considerable thickness cracks are liable to appear as a fresh surface is exposed to the air through carving. As a rule there is no need to worry about them, and they will generally close up again in time. Even should they not do so they are natural to the material and are not likely to detract seriously from the work. At the same time one does not want cracks if they can be avoided, and, where the carving admits, it is a good plan to have a hole (one inch or so in diameter) bored down the centre of any large work in the round. This tends to neutralize the effect which the atmosphere would have if it acted only on the outside of the wood. For a similar reason, the back may be hollowed out of a figure which is to be fixed permanently against a wall or in a niche.

Where a large crack is a nuisance while the actual carving is in process, it may be found helpful to fill it with beeswax. The wax should be pressed in while soft and cleaned off as soon as it is hard. This unites the two sides and prevents the edges from breaking or splintering. The beeswax remains as a filling after the carving is finished, and never becomes so hard that it cannot be squeezed out by the two sides of the crack coming together again should they tend to do so. Never stop a natural crack with a slip of wood: if such a crack wishes to close up it must be free to do so or something disruptive will occur elsewhere. On the other hand, where an opening occurs at an artificial joint, it may be filled with a thin wedge-shaped slip of the same wood. In the latter case there is not the same irresistible force to be encountered should the two sides incline to come together again. Knot-holes and blemishes of a like nature may be filled with plastic wood. This is a quick-drying preparation of cellulose and wood pulp, and is bought in tubes and tins from ironmongers and tool shops. It sets hard and can be worked with any sort of tool, and painted or stained with any sort of medium.

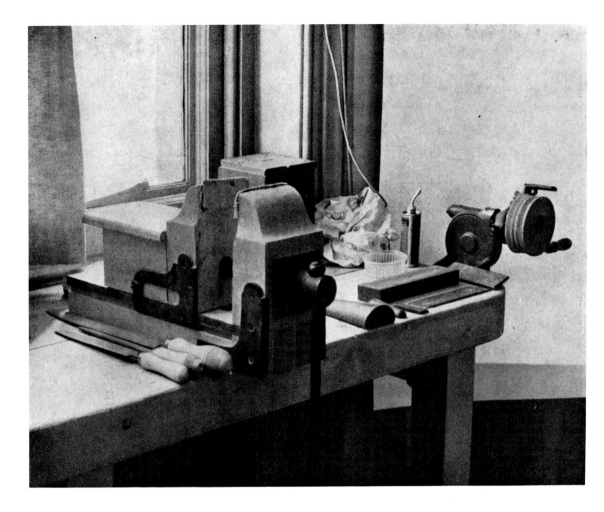

THE BENCH AND ITS EQUIPMENT

A carver's bench must be solidly constructed, and it must stand firmly on the floor. This shows a part of the bench in my studio. It is twenty inches wide, and the top is made of two deal planks three inches thick. The legs are three inches by three inches, and the total height is three feet two inches. At intervals of two feet it has holes bored in it, three inches from the edge and one inch in diameter. These are used to attach the wooden vice, shown in the plate, which is held in place by a screw that goes down through the bench and has a butterfly nut and washer underneath. The holes can also be used for a bench screw, that is a screw about eight inches long which may be used for holding one's carving in place. The point of the screw is inserted into the

24

work, the other end passed downwards through the hole in the bench, a wooden washer slipped on to this from underneath and screwed tight with a butterfly nut. The bench should, when possible, be at least five feet long.

The wooden vice is very useful for holding work of all kinds. The jaws, which open to ten inches, are faced with strips of cork and felt so that they grip without bruising. It can be used for quite large work, which need not be held entirely by the vice, but can rest with one end upon the bench and the other gripped in the jaws of the vice.

The curved and tapering stone shown in the plate, nearest to the vice, is the India slip. This has one side convex and the other concave, and the edges are rounded. It is so made that a curve to fit both the inside and outside of most gouges, except the very small ones, can be found on some part of its surface. The largest stone shown is the Washita oilstone; the others are various slips for the smaller tools.

At the end of the bench is a highly-geared carborundum grindstone, four inches in diameter, which cuts very quickly. The surface should be smooth and not worn into grooves; the one shown has become worn with long service (such grooves may be very useful, for they fit the gouges used upon them—but this is not an orthodox method of grinding tools).

The little glass near the oil-can is for water, into which the tool must be constantly dipped when it is being ground, or it will get over-heated and the temper will be destroyed.

On the near side of the vice are three wood-rasps. These, with files and rifflers of various kinds, are very useful tools—when employed in the right way and in the right place. At times they can be almost indispensable. But they *can* be very destructive in the hands of anyone who has not sufficient experience to enable him to feel the quality of his material. I would strongly advise a beginner not to attempt to make use of any kind of rasping or rubbing technique until he has learned to get the shapes he aims at with cutting tools alone—that is, until he knows he can carve. I mention these implements here in order to give this warning.

Other things that will be needed are cramps (say, a pair of six-inch iron and a pair of six-inch wooden); saw; hammer and nails; screwdriver and screws; gimlet; glue (the ordinary solid or powder glue, melted in a glue-pot, is the strongest; but a prepared liquid glue in a tin will serve in many instances and may be more handy); a plane and spokeshave; and all sorts of oddments of wood for wedges, stops etc—but all these things accumulate of themselves.

3. How to use a tool with the mallet.

HOLDING THE TOOLS

During the all-important stage in a carving known as 'bosting-in', that is knocking the work into shape, one or other of the larger gouges is used in conjunction with the mallet. The tool is held in the left hand with the thumb along the handle, as shown in Plate 3. This position of the thumb steadies the tool and prevents its slipping round in the hand, especially when the latter becomes hot and sweaty.

In order to get the first feel of the tools and mallet, any handy piece of wood, wedged firmly, so that it cannot wobble, may be practised upon. Care should be taken not to hold the body rigid. Wrists and elbows must be as free and unconstrained as possible. One has to grow as unconscious of the tools one uses as of one's knife and fork.

After some practice at striking the tool correctly with the mallet, using varying degrees of strength, the hands may be reversed: the tool being held in

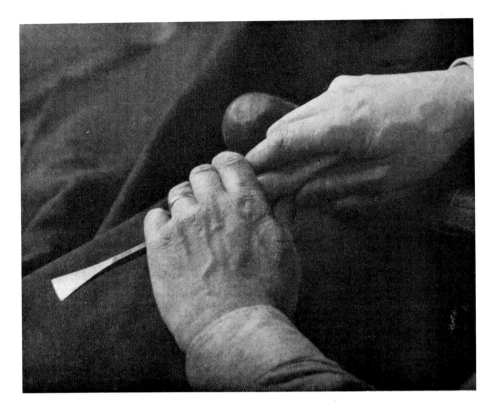

4. How to hold a tool when not using the mallet.

the right hand and the mallet in the left. It is extremely useful in carving to be ambidextrous, and this practised from the start may save a great deal of trouble later on.

In Plate 4 is illustrated the way to hold the tool when not using the mallet. The right hand is over the end of the handle and the left hand, lightly clasped, steadies the upper part of the blade and controls it. This is the way to finish off as a general rule; though there are times, at all stages of a carving, when it is preferable to use the mallet, even with the smaller tools. Without the mallet one gains in sensitiveness: with it there is more control and less likelihood of making slips.

The spade-shaped tool, shown in this plate, is for finishing off. This type of tool is not strong enough for very heavy work; but it may be used with a mallet, or tapped with the lower part of the right hand when a little extra control is needed.

Carving a Relief

THE BULL

In the introduction I undertook to show how, from the outset, a beginner might work from his own design. With this end in view I have carved the relief shown in Plates 5 to 9. It represents one of the Signs of the Zodiac—the Bull. I have chosen one out of a universally known series, not so that it may be copied, but that anyone who cares to do so may try his hand at a parallel piece, following my description step by step, but making use of another of the Signs. They offer great variety—ranging from the simple device of the Scales, through the Crab and the Scorpion and the higher forms of animal life, the Ram and the Goat, to the human figure, both male and female.

The treatment, size and measurements are matters for individual choice; but for the material I would recommend lime or sycamore, or a wood of that nature—not oak.

A sense of purpose may be gained from the beginning, and the imagination stimulated, if one supposes the panel to be intended to form part of a decorative scheme for the library of an observatory—or some such fancy.

Material: plane wood. Size of panel: one foot four inches long, one foot high, two inches thick.

Problem. To carve the bull so that the total thickness of relief is one inch, of which one-half inch stands out from the front face of the panel: that is to say, the main surface of the panel must be cut back one-half inch, and then the background must be hollowed out a farther one-half inch within the boundary of the oval line. The figure ♉ (the conventional sign for the Bull) is to be left raised one-eighth inch at each corner of the panel.

Plate 5. The design is here drawn on the block in charcoal. It is generally advisable to make preliminary sketches and drawings on paper so as to avoid erasures and alterations on the wood itself.

Having drawn the design, the next thing is to fix the panel in position for carving. There are various ways of holding one's work firmly. In the illustration on page 30 small wooden blocks are nailed to the bench, close up to the panel on three sides; against the lower side, nearest to the camera, there is a strip of wood which is held to the bench by a cramp. This strip can

5. The design for the relief carving drawn on to the wood.

be seen (though not very clearly) at the bottom right-hand corner, and one of the small blocks is more evident on the left-hand side.

Another way is to screw on to the panel, from the back, a board which projects an inch or so all round; using, say, four screws, which are long enough to penetrate into the panel about one-half inch. Then the board, not the panel, can be clamped to the bench or screwed upright to the wall.

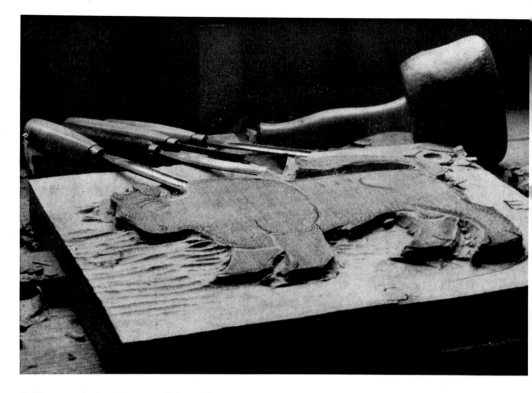

6. The panel after the central figure has been 'set in' and the background reduced.

Or the work may be simply clamped to a corner of the bench, using two cramps at diagonally opposite corners of the panel. In this latter case a slip of wood must be placed between the cramp and the face of the carving to avoid bruising the surface.

The method used in the illustration is the most satisfactory when the panel is of a symmetrical shape that can be lifted out of the blocks and re-placed, top for bottom, when it is necessary: there are no cramps sticking up to get in the way of any part of the surface.

When once the panel is fixed, carving can be started. The main surface has to come down so as to leave the animal projecting one-half inch above it, but the conventional signs at the four corners must be left one-eighth inch above this reduced surface.

30

I hope that anyone who looks carefully at the plates will have no difficulty in seeing how it is done—and then be able to carve something of the same nature himself.

Plate 6. In the thickness of the panel, draw a line all round, three-eighths inch from the top. Then with gouge D or fluter K (see Plate 1), preferably using the mallet, outline the bull; follow this outline with one of the larger gouges, C, just outside the small groove made by D or K. With the same gouge C commence to cut down the surface, working from the outer edges into the deep groove round the animal, and being careful not to go below the line drawn in the thickness of the panel. From time to time it will be necessary to 'set in' the central carving: that is to say, with flat F held perpendicularly to the surface, strike sharply downwards with the mallet at the outline of the bull. By doing this, rough ends of wood are cleaned off, and the background is reduced close up to the central figure. In 'setting in' care must always be taken not to undercut. After the main surface has been cut down with the gouge, it must be smoothed off. This is done with the various flats, sometimes with, sometimes without, the mallet. In all wood-carving the direction of the grain plays an important part. As can easily be seen in the illustration, the grain in this instance runs nearly straight across the carving. As a general rule it is easier to work diagonally across the grain, whenever possible. When cutting *with* the grain great care must be taken that the tool does not go too deep and the wood split. This tendency will be found when the direction of the grain, though nearly straight, runs slightly towards the centre—or into the carving. When this happens, it is advisable to reverse the whole panel so as to cut more easily from the opposite direction. The feel of the wood quickly tells the direction in which one can work with safety. At the end of the first exercise the main surface of the panel should be smoothly reduced by three-eighths inch, leaving the central figure untouched.

Next, mark off one-eighth inch below the first line on the sides of the panel. Draw the conventional sign in each corner; outline these with the fluter, or by setting them in; cut down the surface around them by one-eighth inch, using whichever gouge seems most suitable; and smooth off as before. The end of the second exercise should leave the total surface reduced by one-half inch, on which the signs are raised one-eighth inch, the central figure being still untouched. Progress can be readily recorded through carving the four similar signs one after the other. A careful study of Plate 6 will, I hope, make clear the explanation of these two preliminary exercises.

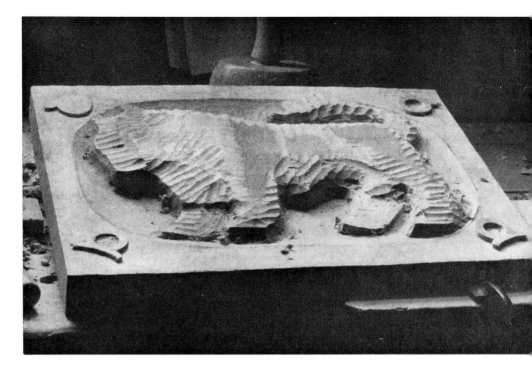

7. Here the oval surround has been recessed, and the central carving strongly 'bosted in'.

Plate 7. Draw in the oval line surrounding the bull, and with, say, gouge 'G' and the mallet, work from this line, saucerwise, towards the centre. Set in the animal as necessary until there is a depth of one inch below the body. When the background is cleared away, bost-in the central carving strongly, cutting down first those parts which must be in lowest relief, such as the off legs. The sooner the surface is broken up the better, so that the mind may be freed from all sense of two-dimensional drawing. Do not be afraid of taking away too much; everyone at first has the opposite tendency. In carving it is far better always to work with decision, and sometimes make mistakes, than to play for safety with tentative little chips.

Plate 8. Here the carving is shown nearing completion. After the main planes have been broadly shaped with a gouge, they must be trued up. Make as certain as possible that the different parts are in their right relation to each other before attempting to get a finished surface. If, for instance, one is rather

8. The carving near completion, the main planes having been broadly shaped with a gouge.

satisfied with an ear, it requires some effort to cut it away in order to carve it again farther in. Think all the time of the shapes, and the hands will automatically guide the tool into doing the right thing. It is the contours and sections which matter more than the bounding lines. The slightest curve will look full and satisfying provided it is true in section—but not otherwise. In a relief one should invariably make full use of the thickness of material available for each part. If the design does not always admit of this, the design is at fault. Be careful never to finish up with a shallow carving on the top of a sort of cliff, with the background down below.

It is advisable to finish a relief in a vertical position with a side light; or, when possible, with the lighting as nearly as may be that in which it is ultimately to be seen. In Plate 8 the panel is resting on a fixed ledge, or shelf, against the wall of the studio, and is held by a wooden clamp pressing on the lower left-hand corner.

9. The finished work.

Plate 9. This shows the finished work. It is a very simple carving and required very few tools—perhaps six in all.

It must be understood that the method, as here described, of working in successive and separate stages is intended to give progressive lessons to a beginner. As will be found by experience, much greater freedom is gained when the work is allowed to grow *as a whole* from start to finish—dispensing as far as possible with all arbitrary measurements.

For instance learn from the start to trust your hand and eye; and in drawing the oval round the bull and placing the four ♉ signs, do not rely on rulers or dividers. The quality of free-hand and the confidence it implies will give life to all your work. But let me repeat what has been said elsewhere, where an architectural setting is concerned exact measurements must be made—and checked.

34

Carving in the Round

THE DRUMMER

Great as are the possibilities of work in relief, it does not wholly satisfy one whose instinct for sculpture has been aroused through the fascination of actually carving. He feels the urge to do something in the round, free-standing and independent of background—something which fills a place in space.

The technical equipment needed for this remains very much the same as for a relief; but, whereas the latter can always be referred, more or less, to a two-dimensional drawing, a work in the round requires the ability to form, and to hold, a mental image in three dimensions. This will at first be found difficult, except in the very simplest cases.

It will probably be best, therefore, for any beginner, when once he has an initial idea in his head, to make a rough sketch model in clay or in modelling wax. This will be a guarantee against what he eventually achieves being something quite different from what he originally intended; it will also ensure that the design will fit into the material available. The model, however, should be set aside as soon as possible; and it should never be used as an exact copy for the work itself.

With practice, and above all with self-reliance, the making of a model may even be dispensed with entirely. Then such preliminary notes as are required can be done on paper, and the design drawn in chalk or charcoal directly on to the material itself.

I do not wish to be misleading on this point, which is of importance. It would obviously be foolish for anyone not to have recourse to a sketch model at any time when he felt it would be a real help to him. It is a matter for individual discretion. But I do regard it as vital that a *modelled design* should not form the basis of a work of carving, to the extent that the carving becomes in fact little more than a reproduction or copy of the modelled design. The mind alone shapes the material, and the hands which guide the tools should be free to follow the mental image.

The illustrations on pages 36 to 43 show the process of carving a figure in the round.

10. *THE FIRST STAGE*
A diagrammatic drawing.

A. side view.
B. front view.

36

11. The chalk outline on the block, with arrows indicating saw-cuts.

12. The waste wood cut away with the large gouge.

Material: teak. Dimensions of block: two feet by ten inches by eight inches.

Problem. To carve a figure standing securely on its own feet, without base or other attachment.

Plate 10. The first stage. After a number of sketches and scribbles, through which the design takes shape, a diagrammatic drawing is made on paper, within an outline of the block itself, showing two points of view—'A' the side and 'B' the front. These drawings are intentionally kept thin, as all forms tend to become fuller when translated from two dimensions to three. They are, in fact, little more than the skeleton of the design.

Plate 11. The second stage. On each side of the block an outline taken from 'A' is drawn in chalk. The arrows indicate points at which saw-cuts will be made.

Plate 12. The third stage. The block is sawn down to the chalk line at the four points indicated by arrows. It is then laid on its front on the bench with its top end up against a stop, probably a wooden clamp. The grain runs lengthwise and is very straight. The waste wood is quickly cut away with the largest gouge and the mallet; working from the heel to the saw-cut at the waist; from the elbow to the top; and (in the opposite direction) from the elbow to the saw-cut at the waist. It will be noticed in the plate that a small additional saw-cut has been made behind the knee. The block is turned over and the opposite side is treated in a similar manner. The tool-marks in the illustration say all that is necessary.

Then an approximate outline taken from 'B' in Plate 10 is drawn, as well as the roughened surface will admit, on the front and back of the block; saw-cuts are made as seem advisable, and the waste wood is again cut away—though the block is left intact for two inches or so at the base.

During this process the block is unattached. When it becomes too irregular in shape to lie unsupported on the bench, it may be held in the vice, or steadied in some way with cramps or wedges.

As soon as the waste wood is gone, the work is ready to be fixed to the bench or turn-table. The method here used is that which I have found by far the most satisfactory for carvings of small or middle size: all those, that is to say, which are not heavy enough to stand firmly by their own weight.

A solidly built deal table three feet six inches high has a fixed top eighteen inches square. Above this is a revolving top having a central wooden pin, two inches in diameter, which goes down through a hole in the fixed top. The

38

THE FOURTH STAGE
13. The carving after the first bosting-in.

revolving top is made up of an oak board twenty inches square and one-half inch thick, with a framework of deal, two inches wide and one-half inch thick, on the underside, which bears on the fixed top.

The work is placed on the table in a convenient position, preferably with its front flush with one edge of the top. A line is drawn round the work which is then lifted off. Three points within this line, forming as large a triangle as possible and having regard to where the screw-holes will come in relation to the carving, are selected; and holes are bored with a gimlet. The revolving top is then lifted off. The work is stood on its head on the floor, held perhaps between the knees, or by someone else, and the reversed table-top is placed over its base in such a way that the base comes exactly within the drawn line. A bradawl is stuck into the base through each in turn of the holes already made, so as to mark it. The table-top is lifted away and screw-holes are started with the gimlet at each of these marks in the base. The table-top is replaced and screwed on to the work from underneath with three two-inch screws. Then the table-top with the work attached is lifted up and let down into its place on the table. It is advisable to make a note of exactly where the screws are, for guidance in the later stages of the carving. The work is now securely fixed to the table, and can be turned about at will.

Plate 13. The fourth stage. This shows the carving at an early but all-important stage. In the first bosting-in the work is committed, for better or worse, to the essentials of its design—to the interrelation of its various parts upon which its movement and vitality must ultimately depend.

It generally feels natural to start carving from the top and to work downwards: certainly in this case it is necessary to find at the outset such points as the top of the head and the shoulders from which the uncovering process, which carving fundamentally is, can commence. When once such salient points have been fixed, all other parts can be referred to them, in a way which I think can be more easily grasped through a study of the illustration than by any attempt at a verbal explanation. The actual finding of the head depends on the ability to visualize the figure in the block, but the position has been approximately defined by the cutting away of all the waste wood from side to side and from front to back.

When once a decision has been made, carving should be started strongly with one of the larger gouges and the mallet.

Work *round* each part, cutting across the grain, always concentrating on the form to be uncovered however far that form may be below the surface that

Charcoal marks for central lines
are helpful guides at all stages.

14 and 15. The figure gradually emerges.

has been reached. Deliberate from time to time upon what is to be done next —and then do it swiftly and systematically. At every stage of a carving the tool-marks show whether the work is going well or badly: whether the directing thought is clear or muddled. Do not try to take off more with each cut than the tool can manage. It is a good rule to aim at keeping at least one point of the gouge always in view. Should the tool become buried and stuck in the wood, do not attempt to release it by wriggling it about, for then it is almost certain to snap off. Leave it where it is; and, taking another tool, cut away the wood very carefully in front of the one which is stuck. It will soon become free enough to be gently drawn out.

Plates 14 and 15. These show the figure gradually emerging. Holes have appeared between the body and the arms, and the wood has been cut away between the legs; though not down to the feet where the screws are holding. Very often a drill is helpful for piercing holes, but in this instance they have arrived through carving round each part until it detached itself.

As the work gets nearer to the finished surface it becomes increasingly necessary to think of it in section. Try to imagine what would be shown by a saw-cut through each part—across the forehead, the chest; through the waist, the arm, the calf—and consider whether each separate form is true and expressive, or indeterminate and meaningless. Good sculpture is, essentially, a good shape made up of a combination of good shapes harmoniously related so as to form a single harmonious whole.

Various charcoal marks will be noticed in Plate 14—down the centre line, across the brow etc. Such guides are very helpful at all stages of a carving. They should be put in freehand, without recourse to callipers or other measuring instrument. The hand and eye will work with the exact degree of accuracy which a work of art asks for—provided the artist will trust to them implicitly. Of course, this does not apply where mathematically accurate measurements are necessary for such work as is to fit into an architectural setting, or to questions of that nature.

As shown in Plate 15, 'E', 'F' and 'I' are the tools used at this stage for truing up and finishing off. But by the time a beginner has reached a point equivalent to this, he will have decided for himself what tools he wants to use, and when.

When working in the round, even more than in relief, it is necessary to remember the injunction not to be afraid of taking off too much. It is astonishing at first to see what a heap of chips lie on the floor in proportion to the

16. The finished work.

seemingly small impression made on the work itself. Similarly, the amount of cutting which it takes to convert a square section into a round or oval will be found just as astonishing. For this reason the work of nearly all beginners has a tendency to remain rather four-sided instead of achieving the freedom of a thing seen fully in the round.

Be careful not to make any part look as though it were something *applied* to the surface: imagine all forms as growing outwards from within. The nose, for instance, is not a wedge stuck on to a flat face, but a ridge whose sides appear to be carried back over the planes of the cheeks to meet at the back of the head: the eye is a ball within the sphere of the skull.

When the work is practically finished, except for the feet, it is unscrewed from the table. It is then held in the vice, the soles of the feet are marked on the base, and the remaining waste wood is cut away from beneath upwards so as to avoid flushing the edges. The feet themselves, as well as any parts which can only be got at from underneath, are finished off when the work is unattached, or held as most convenient in the vice.

Plate 16. This shows the finished work; unattached and standing firmly on its own feet. In it an attempt has been made to give the idea of marching to the measured roll of the drum, through the fusion of the simplified forms of the drummer and his instrument.

Any amplification, simplification or distortion which explains, summarizes or emphasizes the living form in terms of the inanimate material of a carving is right and inevitable. To a greater or lesser extent these elements have always been present in all true art, of which they are, in effect, the very essence.

On the other hand, every kind of distortion, or abstraction, which, either deliberately, or through incompetence, runs *counter* to the *nature* of the thing suggested, while leaving it recognizable, is 'falsification'; and this, in my opinion, can have no permanent place in art.

Apart from this—and setting aside the merely imitative and trivial—the degree of representation used in a carving is solely a matter of individual style and vision. It is the intensity of feeling behind a carving that gives it value—not the idiom in which it is expressed.

44

Application

The extent to which all forms of art and craftsmanship can be absorbed into present-day life is a question outside the scope of this book.

But as I have suggested in the Preface to this third edition, the more man's interests and surroundings become mechanized, the greater grows the spiritual need for the work of his hands.

I believe this need can best be met by each individual artist and craftsman making the most of such opportunities as come his way, and showing by the quality and skill he puts into his work that the right things really are better so. But they must be the right things, carried out with respect for tradition, but without too much nostalgic harking back to past ages. For instance, it would be foolish to ban the resources of modern joinery when common sense points to their use.

It must be accepted that the present day is characterized by works of scientific engineering. This is becoming increasingly true of architecture as well as the more obvious building of ships, aeroplanes, bridges, dams and what-not—which all owe their qualities—often magnificent qualities—to science and not to aesthetics. This greatly limits the scope for the employment of art: for it has yet to be proved that science and art can be associated satisfactorily. Yet it is the humanistic interest and personal appeal—which science lacks and art alone can supply—which must be encouraged if humanity itself is not to undergo some form of mechanization.

But a student who has his future to think of will want to know what in these circumstances are the opportunities that may come his way; and, should he take up wood-carving seriously, what chances would he have of getting worth-while jobs? The answer to that question must, of course, rest with each individual. But assuming the ability and a certain amount of enterprise to be there, the illustrations of contemporary work at the end of this book may be found heartening. Though they were not selected with that end in view, they do show, for the most part, works which were commissioned in the first place, or which have subsequently been acquired for public galleries or private collections. They are not all on the scale of the giant figures of Gog and Magog (page 69) which David Evans carved for Guildhall in the heart of the City of London; but there are various other works of importance, notably among those for churches, for which the opening appears to be increasing. There are, for instance, the author's work for the bomb-damaged Cathedral at Manchester of which the south doorway is shown (page 80); the figures of Church and Synagogue for the chapel of St John's Training College, York (pages 76–77); and the clergy and choir seating for Holy Trinity, Northwood (pages 78–79), this latter representing one of the needs which churches have for their essential furnishings.

But to come to more everyday things which will be the immediate concern of a beginner, there is obviously a constant use for chests, cupboards, stools, settles, log-boxes and things of a like nature which lend themselves to the right kind of decoration. The table-settle (page 56) is a fine example of the use of restrained carving to enhance and emphasize the lines of a well-designed piece of furniture. But it is important to remember that the design of the thing itself must in the first instance be good; and carving is only justified when it is part, or completion of that design. Again, the carving on any object which is intended for use or handling should never make it unfriendly to the touch; on the contrary, the carving should itself invite the hand as much as the eye.

Apart from this it may be that there are some subjects to which wood is particularly sympathetic. The animals of the farm and countryside which William Simmonds has carved with such endearing understanding (page 67) could hardly have been made in any other material, so close are they to their native timbers.

EXAMPLES OF
WOOD CARVING

from 2000 BC *to the present day*

PLOUGH
Height, 9 inches
British Museum, London

In looking at this Egyptian carving it is impossible no[t]
to be struck by the sense of life which has been
achieved by extreme simplification and economy of
means. It seems to sum up the whole slow progress o[f]
the plough through human history; it gives one an
abiding sense of the changelessness of the fundame[ntal]
occupations of mankind to realize that these ploughin[g]
oxen were carved on the banks of the Nile before the[ir]
Israelites were in Egypt.

**STATUETTE OF
IMERET-NEBES**
Leyden, Rijksmuseum van Oudheden

Approximately of the same date as
the plate opposite, this statuette is
remarkable for the anatomical
understanding and vision which it
shows. The subtlety of its
treatment vitalizes the formality of
the Egyptian convention and
gives it freedom.

FIGURE OF A MAN   Height, 3 feet 3 inches   *Victoria and Albert Museum, London*

CAPITAL OF A COLUMN
Chestnut wood, Height 2 feet
Victoria and Albert Museum,
London

his richly decorated capital is from
one of four columns which
originally supported a pulpit at
Salerno. It is widely separated in
origin from the lovely free figure
opposite, but the two works have
this in common—each is entirely
right for wood. Note how every
shape, every fold of drapery
instinctively conforms to the
material. Notice, too, how often
the cut shows as the direct
outcome of some particular tool.
cannot think of any two examples
which illustrate better than these
idamental principle of good carving.

FIGURES *British Museum, London*

Independent of time and place, all straightforward and direct methods of carving tend to produce similar results. These two pieces from remote islands in the Pacific afford interesting comparisons with works of entirely different origin.

The figure from Hawaii (below) at once recalls Etruscan and other archaic work of the Mediterranean races. The setting of the eyes, the planes of the nose and cheeks, the unity of all the features with the skull are an object lesson. It is carved in a soft wood. 1 foot 7 inches high.

The Easter Island figure (ha height 1 foot 5 inches) is st reminiscent of some Europe sculpture of the twelfth cen particularly its resemblance certain type of crucifix.

ANGEL

Oak: height, 2 feet 2 inches
*Victoria and Albert Museum,
London*

This angel has been taken
from an architectural setting,
a roof-beam in an East
Anglian church.
Its chief characteristic is
strength; look especially at
the changes of the planes of
the brow, the compactness
and force of the hands and
arms, the incisiveness of the
wings and drapery.

Hawk and Hare, from a stall in St George's Church, Stowlangtoft, Suffol.

MISERICORDS Throughout the Middle Ages choir stalls afforded great scope for wood carving. Whatever the subject, whether sacred or secular, satirical or fancifu the design was invariably appropriate to the shape and space to be filled.
Reproduced by courtesy of Norman Adlard & Co, Ipswich

The martyrdom of St Edmund from a stall in St Andrew's Church, Norton, Suffolk

ANGEL GABRIEL

This angel is from an
Annunciation group.
Originally painted and
[...], it retains a great part
[...] its colour: but so right is
[...]rving that this scarcely
[...]ks the quality of the oak
[...]neath. Particularly to be
[...]ticed is the treatment of
[...] the wings, the hands and
[...] hair. Compare this with
[...] English angel, page 53;
[...]ne is more graceful—the
[...] is stronger; but each is
[...] right in its own way that
[...]y can only be contrasted
[...]or divergent excellencies.

Oak: height, 3 feet *Victoria and Albert Museum, London*

TABLE-SETTLE
Oak: length 5 feet 11 inches
Victoria and Albert Museum, London

The noble roof on the opposite page is typical of many which are to be seen throughout Norfolk and Suffolk. They are the work of a school of East Anglian joiners and carpenters which enriched, principally, the churches of the fifteenth century. Note how inevitable seem the rows of carved angels in the general structural design. This quality of appropriate carving enhancing the design of the object which it adorns is also well illustrated in the seventeenth-century table-settle above.

DOUBLE HAMMER BEAM ROOF in Needham Market, Suffolk

JAMES,
DUKE OF YORK
Boxwood
Victoria and Albert
Museum

This lively little seventeenth-
century statuette is very true
to the hard boxwood
from which it is carved.

Jacopa della Quercia
(1347–1436)

MADONNA AND CHILD
Louvre, Paris

This gracious Italian group
has not the tradition of wood
behind it. It comes from a
marble-carving country.
Compare the texture of the
features and hands and the
rather 'ropey' drapery with
the corresponding quality of
plates on pages 50, 53 and 55.

PULPIT   Church of St Mildred, Bread Street, City of London
(Sir Christopher Wren) destroyed by enemy action, 1940

St Mildred's was, perhaps,
the most complete and least
altered of all the Wren
churches. To many who kne
it, it was for this reason the
most loved.

Church of St Lawrence Jewry, Cheapside, City of
London (also a Wren church destroyed in 1940).
This plate shows in detail how irreplaceable have been
the losses which the English heritage suffered during
the Second World War.

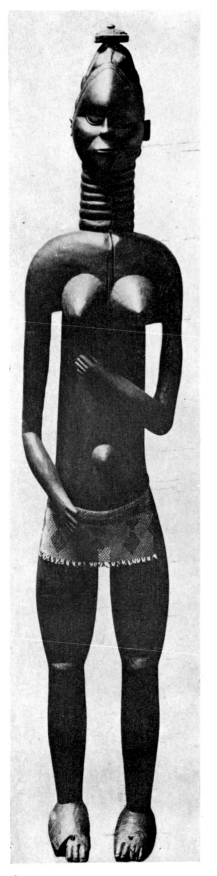

PRIMITIVE AFRICAN

The head, the neck and the
legs of this figure have a lovely
quality and true sculptural
feeling.
The torso may not be
so good, and the arms and
hands have definitely worked
out badly.
These inconsistencies are
often present in primitive
work; a fact to which
enthusiasm blinds some people
who have not themselves had
experience of direct carving.

AMERICAN INDIAN

HOUSE-POST

from Vancouver Island,
mid-nineteenth century.
A fine bold carving with a
feeling of structural fitness
reminiscent of a ship's figure-
head in the days of sail.

E. J. Clack, FRBS

MOTHER AND CHILD
Yew, 6 feet high:
courtesy: *Wood*

W. Soukop, ARA

STANDING WOMAN
Elm, 7 feet high

In these two large figures it is
of interest to note how each
sculptor has made use of the
natural growth of the tree
trunk to the point that he
needed it; but neither has
allowed this to compromise
the unity of the work as a
whole.
Contrast also the lovely
treatments of the heads.

Anne Strauss

THE TREE
Cedar wood:
height 2 feet 6 inches
The charm of Anne Strauss's
work is well shown in this
carving. The numerous
piercings are skilfully con-
trived, and the tree and the
human figures attain complete
unity of design.

(right)
Sir Charles Wheeler, PPRA

MOTHER AND CHILD
Lime-tree trunk:
height 6 feet

The compactness of this
design in no way gives it a
sense of compression. The
figures grow freely within
the limits of the tree trunk,
of whose nature they partake
while expressing the
tenderness of their human
relationship.

Edna Manley

RACHEL
Mahogany,
approximately half life-size

Edna Manley lives in Jamaica, and most of her works are carved out of the wonderful woods which grow on the island. The dignity and grace of *Rachel* the outcome of the artist's vision combined with technical ability. Notice the lean sweep of the lines and the beautiful surface finish, which emphasizes the truth of the underlying forms.

Maurice Lambert, RA

SHOAL OF FISH
Yew
Length, 2 feet 6 inches
Collection of Miss Rebecca West

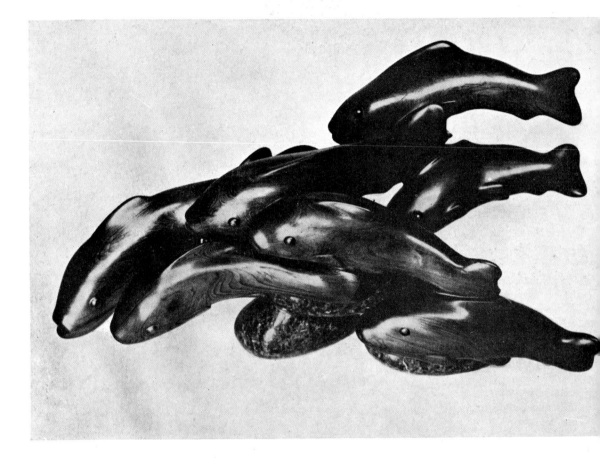

Good sculpture is a good shape made up of a combination of good shapes rightly related to each other. In this the whole piece in its unity is first seen; afterwards the eye can appreciate the individual fish in their lovely grouping. The smoothness—so appropriate for the subject—brings out the flowing grain of the yew wood.

William G. Simmonds, RWA
YOUNG HARE
English oak; length 9 inches

The deep feeling for the animals of
the farm and countryside is
here expressed through the love of
wood-carving executed with matchless skill.

AUTUMN CALF
Carved oak, painted; length 14 inches
Cheltenham Art Gallery

67

Douglas Wain-Hobson
AVE MARIA

Birchwood;
height 2 feet 6 inches
This sensitive carving was
done by Douglas Wain-
Hobson at the Royal College
of Art, London, on his
return there as a student in
1946. The Madonna has a
quiet dignity which looks
confidently to the future while
backed by true tradition.

David Evans, FRBS

MAGOG

One of a pair of giant figures 9 feet 6 inches high *Gog* and *Magog* have been carved from built-up lime-wood and decorated according to tradition, to take their place in Guildhall, London, on its restoration after bomb damage.

69

Ossip Zadkine

ORPHEUS
Elm-tree trunk
Height, 12 feet
Musée de L'Art Moderne, Paris

This colossal figure was carved out
of the trunk of an elm tree. The
whole conception is big and
impressive, quite apart from its
actual size. In detail the design is
full of interest, with its curious
and arresting concave surfaces where
one would normally expect them
to be convex—a convention very
characteristic of this artist's work.

John Skeaping, R A

BLOOD HORSE
White pine wood
Approximately life-size
Collection of Sir Michael Sadler, K.C.S.I.

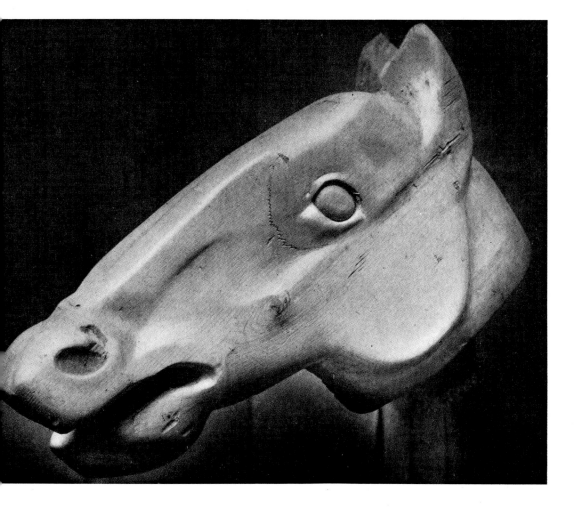

Great knowledge and understanding of the nature of a horse are shown in this stimulating carving. It is a true *translation* of the essential characteristics of nature into terms of the sculptured material, and illustrates very clearly the difference in vitality that exists between this and the superficial *imitation* of the more ordinary vision.

71

Leon Underwood

AFRICAN MADO
Lignum vitae with
silver-gilt inlay and
crown. Height, 4 feet
*Rozetenville School of
Arts and Crafts,
Johannesburg*

A sculptor is often asked which came first, the idea or the material? In other words, did he think of something he wanted to do and then go and look for the material in which to do it, or did some piece of wood or stone which he already had by him suggest how it should be carved?

The African Madonna was commissioned for a native School of Arts and Crafts in South Africa. It was carved from a 6 cwt. log of lignum vitae.

Accepting the possibilities and limitations of this very hard tropical wood Leon Underwood ha achieved great freedom in the swing and vigour of his forceful group.

Toma Rosandić

TORSO
Walnut
Approximately life size
Collection of Mr F. M. S. Winand

In the case of this female torso I think there can be no doubt that the figure was suggested to Rosandic by the curved bole of a walnut tree which he already had.

He has used his opportunity finely: the carving is entirely free; there is no suggestion of constraint: no feeling that the design was anywhere conditioned by lack of material.

THE SEA BIRD
Pear wood
Height, 2 feet
Collection of Mrs Philip Samuel

SHOE-BILL STORK
Ebony
Height, 2 feet
Ebony is perhaps the hardest and most tricky of all
woods; but the quality is lovely. The contrast of the
sap-wood, also very hard, has been used in the design.

ST MARY from a group The Annunciation. Oak
This group was acquired for Winchester Cathedral in 1944 and has been placed in the north transept.

left, **CHURCH**
right, **SYNAGOGUE**
Oak
each 3 feet 6 inches high.
facing page: The Chapel,
St John's College, York,
with the figures shown
in situ
Architect:
George Pace FRIBA

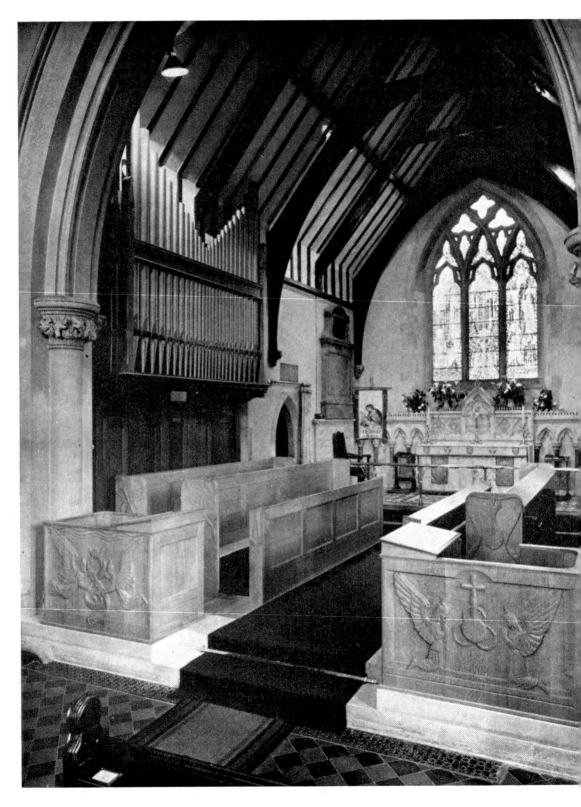

Examples of the Author's Work

opposite: Clergy and choir
stalls in Holy Trinity,
Northwood, Middlesex.
English oak
left: **PRAYER**
one of two carvings on the
clergy stall at the entrance
to the chancel; a matching
carving represents *Praise*.
below: details of the choir
stalls, which carry the
musical instruments
mentioned in the Bible.

79

South Door of Manchester
Cathedral with
THE GOOD SHEPHERD
Architect: Sir Hubert
Worthington, RA, MA, FRIBA
above Detail of the carving
English oak
Length, 6 feet 2 inches